Sex, Death, and Naked Men

[signature: Bernice Friesen]

Bernice Friesen

Sex, Death, and Naked Men

To Paul,

Joy + Luck!

Berni

+Hornby Garden tour
June 30 2018

COTEAU BOOKS

Edited by Elizabeth Philips.

Cover and book design by Duncan Campbell.

Cover illustration, "Mister Screaming Pants " by Bernice Friesen.
Author photograph by R. Cain, Hornby Island, B.C.
Interior illustrations, by Bernice Friesen, are drawings of one of Michelangelo's
Dying Slaves in the Louvre, Paris, and of the sculpture of Apollo from the
west pediment of the Temple of Zeus, Olympia, Greece.

Printed and bound in Canada.

The publisher gratefully acknowledges the financial assistance of the
Saskatchewan Arts Board, the Canada Council for the Arts,
the Department of Canadian Heritage, and the City of Regina
Arts Commission, for its publishing programme.

Coteau Books celebrates the 50th anniversary of
the Saskatchewan Arts Board with this publication.

Canadian Cataloguing in Publication Data

Friesen, Bernice, 1966
Sex, death, and naked men

Poems.
ISBN 1-55050-140-2

1. Title.
PS8561.R4952 S48 1998   C811'.54   C98-920121-X
PR9199.3.F75 S48 1998

Coteau Books
401-2206 Dewdney Avenue
Regina, Saskatchewan
S4R 1H3

AVAILABLE IN THE U.S. FROM:

General Distribution Services
85 River Rock Road, Suite 202
Buffalo, New York,
USA, 14207

For Colin

Contents

Sex

3   God's Penis
4   Mae West Does Eve
5   Penis Envy at the Dawn of Creation
6   First Apple
7   Wanting in Old Photographs
9   Olympia
16 Red Neck Love
17 The Catch
19 A Medieval Spell Requiring Penance
21 Harem
22 Ovum Poem: Girl Meets Boy
23 Chastity
24 Five Women
26 On the Rag
27 Wait For It

Death

31 Dragon Fly
33 Old Woman With Wings
35 The Railroad in the 1950s
36 Elegy for Maria
37 When
38 St. Helen
39 Women Keep Death
40 Skate
41 The Humours Deranged
44 Where You Are Taking Me
45 Running
46 Breasts and Carcinogens
50 Prairie Woman
52 Fear of Life Taken
54 Leaving the Land / Memory
55 De Medici

Naked Men

63 Nude Model

64 Freud as Adam

65 That Angel Michael Buonarroti With His Red Lamborghini

68 The False Dawn of Mechanics

69 Plato as Adam

70 The Tyger

72 The Popes as Adam

74 Atlas Held Aloft in the Heavens by a Green Orange

75 Rutting Season at the Café

76 Adam, You Little Devil

77 Waitress Honesty

78 Bathing N

80 Darwin as Adam

81 The Son Forsaken in The Garden

82 the begatitudes

83 Him in the Sky

84 My Sister, My Spouse

86 My Father as Adam / Ancestral Memories of The Garden

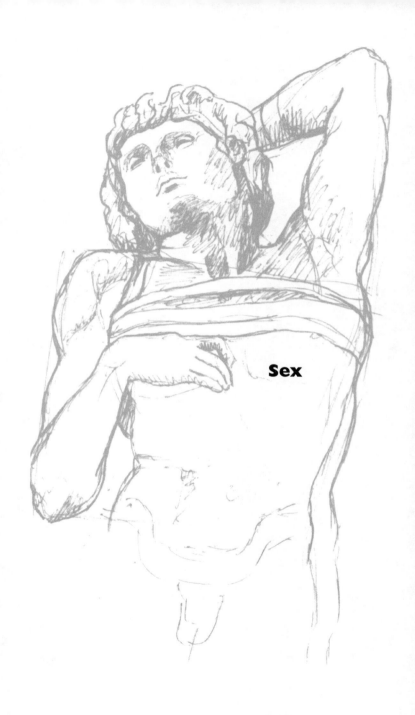

Sex

God's Penis

He finds it eternally funny
Christians have a problem
with His anatomy.

They wanted a male God
yet can't imagine Him actually *using* it

but would God
have a useless appendage?

He smiles, spews forth another
hundred thousand stars.

Mae West Does Eve

Pull a man's penis
and he'll unravel
like a skein of wool.
It was something my mother taught me.

I'll tell you why I found the snake so appealing.
I was just looking for a man who was all dick.
How much fun do you think Adam could have been
before sin was invented?
Oh.

Penis Envy at the Dawn of Creation

Some think it's God
who told 'em how
to do
it,
implanted information –
instinctual information –
kindergarten basics like
how to wipe a bum
how to blow a nose
stand themselves up straight
showed 'em where to put it

but I think they learned it from the slugs.

Long green turds
slinkin' in the grass
have silent slimy battles in their love.
Here reduction
equals reproduction,
a-sex-u-al-i-ty, yin and yang.
Slug bites off
the penis of another:
"Make a woman out of you," he says.
Then they writhe,
examples for reflection
of the mother and the father of us all.

But just remember this
in the first love-making
it was Adam lost the rib
not Eve.

First Apple

You sliced slow curved
wedges, stab, wait
for me to take them
in my mouth
from your
knife, then carved
the core
like a small
totem with seeds
for eyes.

The earth we sit
on is wild
with sun and
shade.
The trees move
and the stone
wall reddens
in the morning
like the apple
skin coiled
at my feet.

Wanting in Old Photographs

You black-gowned boy
graduate
thin red-haired
almost virgin.
On the day of my birth
not a thing in your head
but the Beatles
that hidden part of your body
sensing bare-bellied girls,
long hair rain-running
over their shoulders.

On my tenth birthday you
were a black-and-white terrorist,
bearded, serious, dangerous,
eyes calm before explosions
behind round John Lennon specs,
old German girlfriend already barb-
wiring your heart, laying mines.

And then the day before
I met you, doctor of business,
freckled gentle hands on woolen thigh,
every photo a ghost of yourself
more years stolen by circles of the sun.

I would time-travel to have you
at all ages, eighteen,
twenty-six, forty-three,
taste the back of your teeth,
the blue lines of wrists,
let you find the small bone
at the end of my spine,
and leave.
I'd be one of your free
lovers of the sexual revolution,
look into those eyes that won't know
they will know me.

Olympia

I.

I am on the wrong train
dropped by a broken station
night air of cactus flowers
derailed.

The mountain is a woman.
Olympia, deflowered by shopkeepers
who step on her.
Olympic jewelers, postcard keepers,
the hairy-chested harlots of the Peloponnes
beckon in doorways:
Hi, sweeties.
Their unshaven words
rasp against my cheeks,
insinuate down my ass.

Outdoor tables,
thick, grainy coffee,
baklava, leaves of autumn pastry
crushed, honey falling
slow from this spoon.
Cabbies with bulging pants
shout in the dark, want
to take me for a ride.

II.

Yellow laundry flaps
before a blue storm.
On the mountain
there are lawns.
Busloads of the aged
walk gravel paths
among stones
hewn and tumbled.
They trot the Olympic mile
in windbreakers and
Nikes.

A sign says
Let the Greek Gods show you the way,
but I lose myself, self-guided,
looking for a phone,
my man at home
faint and far away in my ear.

In the cab
Ikyes calls me
a kilometer high
in Greek, silly,
names my watch Sigmund Freud.
He says I am his
because he is the tallest man
and I am taller than them all.

The mountain is a woman.

We pass an Orthodox
priest miming to his wife.
She shakes a rag rug from her balcony.

III.

The older woman from the hostel
walks me through the streets –
tourists pacing October so
out of season.

See the old men, so squat and round?

Caps cover their baldness
as they spend the day on checkers
in white-washed sun,
chickens worming at their shoelaces.

See any women?

*They are at home cutting aubergines,
suckling babies,
or if single, in Athens
with their books.
These can leave the family
because they are not sons –
not important enough
to drive a cab,
support their ancestors.*

I feel sorry for them, she says
as another train spills its tourists

11

and the cabs swarm. *The young men,*
their empty summer feasting:
tall German Brunhildes
blonde American amazons
shorts, backpacks, tanned thighs.

Men go to Thailand
for sex vacations,
women, to Greece for
pure-faced Hellenes,
men who are boys
always.

IV.

I draw Theodykes, Ikyes the cabby,
pen sensuous against paper
earlobe, iris,
temple,
Apollo's nose and brow.
Greek boys mimic the shapes of marble,
look like their fathers
dead two thousand years.

Ikyes, poor baby,
dances with himself
hands hard on my back
stumbling me along for the ride,
his decoration
to impress the boys,
yet another tourist girl
cactus flower
crushed at Zorba's.

You are more beautiful without your glasses.
You say to yourself
          "This Greek man
          is not going to get me."
You're afraid of me.
Where's your heart
Puritan?
I had a tall woman once —
we will be the same height
lying down.

He slips a hand down the
v-back of my shirt and
the boys cheer him on
as he avoids me,
the one who has drawn him,
reproduced what he sees with
breathes with
a woman who already knows
his face too well.

V.

The temple of Zeus
from the west pediment,
the last day of my Olympiad.

Apollo, his arm stretched
naked serpent of bicep
the other arm absent
immaterial, therefore immortal.
His penis is broken off,
immortal.

Drink, friend.
A waiter translates an offer
from a fifty year old man,
grey hair curling up his neck
from the nest of his pectorals.
Locals watch subtitled Tarzan
in restaurants every evening.

The ape man
Tarzan with black curly hair
beating his chest,
wobbling the little roll of fat
wrapping his belly.
How much time
is left on the meter?

Ikyes searches the restaurants,
sends his friends to insist for him,
but I will not go again to Zorba's, not even
remembering the exhale of breath
from between his clothes and skin,
nothing but man and the heat of the day,
a brush through rosemary
at the side of the road.

I tear the drawing from my book.

In a jeweler's window
an armlet snake lies
in velvet. I want
it to coil around my thighs,
a lock of Medusa
to turn one of us to stone.

VI.

Olympia, green hill,
verdant breast.
There are columns
of fluted marble
quaked down to
domino lines of tumbled wheels,
fat stones pierced
to insert an iron rod
dissolved now
by rust, rain, bombardment.
String a needle with boulders.

Ikyes will be out there, waiting
on my last night
at the door of the hostel
which crouches behind shops,
places of yogurt,
moussaka, oranges,
threads of wheat soaked in honey.
He will beg for me to use him
just a little, though phrased
with machismo
so the youths may cheer.

I could have left yesterday
but the place is too thick with pity and lust
and he knows it.
I go to the temple again,
sit on the avalanche of civilization.

Red Neck Love

Blackbird wavers from cat tail.
Four-by-four buckshot with rust
snap of gravel
aspen trembling shadows
on dust
on windows.

They spread the muscled lips
of barbed wire
and pass through
with black soled feet.

Sun finds them in the grass
while irradiating oats
foxtail.
The blades emboss her spine
his knees.
A blinking steel tower
the relay of microwaves above them.

The stubble field
beyond is the penitential
bed of nails. Hammerheaded
wells pump oil.
A wick of methane
burns the air.

The Catch

1.

White boat on a lake.
Islands of dry rushes
over a man-flooded forest,
trees harpooning up
from the weeds. After

hours, he pulls
his long penis into
the sun to urinate, far
from shore, an arc
amber against sky,

water. She watches.
No fish here in Fishing
Lake, only water
striders, boat men,
damsel flies, maiden head.

"They won't bite.
The fish, they know
about lines and lures."
He takes her to the
boat bottom, wool

blanket scratching her
shoulders. Taut, he
pierces her, the punch
of a needle. Her pain
cries him out of her

and they lie together
with blood, the smell
of scales, waves thrumming
the boat like the tails of jack.

2.

She sits in his bath that night
white enamel, mouth-
hollow, hot water lapping
up the damp under
breast, skin hot on skin.

Tendrils of sex rise
out of her, mucous weeds
thread through milty soap
water, wet rafts of sperm and
semen, larvae floating, algae.

She slides down, under, opens
her eyes below the surface,
watches him unzip, pinching
her lips, then eyes, against
hot water, everything.

A Medieval Spell Requiring Penance

I'm one of those women
who strips off her jeans,
French knickers,
spreads herself with honey
and rolls in a carpet of wheat
on the kitchen floor
like those cone-hatted babes
who danced the maypole
in the year one thousand.
Solidarity with witchy feminists everywhere.

The problems are eternal,
not just sticky flour
in the clogged throat of the electric mill,
wheat and honey in the pubic hairs,
sweet folds of ear and vulva.

"What have you been up to?"
the boyfriend asks.

And what if you forget
to shut the venetians
and the Venetians look in

or the sewer man is knocking to
ream out your pipes, or worse,

Jehovah's Witnesses find the door unlocked
and there you are
bare, sticky and granulated.
If they offer you a leaflet do you take it?
Do you argue doctrine
sitting around the dining room table?

If you're serious about this business,
bake the bawdy body meal
into a medieval cake
and any man who eats it
will lust to taste the soles of your hands,
palms of your feet.

He'll dance the pavane naked
if you ask him
in front of his mother,
the local sex-role zealots,
then cook you macaroni and cheese
from scratch.

Then say to him, "Have another.
This is from my lower
lip, the nape of my
thighs, those two dimples that nestle
above my dear sweet fanny."

He'll sell his goats
to buy you orchids, love birds, Chanel,
even in times when a female slave was a unit of measure
worth three chickens and change.

Harem

A nestle of ova
in their fibrous fleshy bed.
Ovary
hatchery
spermery
monastery.
Contemplative little Buddhist eggs.

They can handle the odd orgasm.
Those regular floods of
hormones are their only gripe.
Most just get bitchy,
but see – a sister swells,
grows addle-pated,
reads Harlequins,
and the next thing you know,
Pop!
she goes completely down the tubes.

Gelatinous, shaken, they develop
a mythology of death
and the after birth,
bloody oblivion for all
but the elect

who shiver the mind-
blowing coupling of gametes,
thigh-clasp of RNA and RNA,
two become one until
the cell splitting
becomes the hum of life
a multiple personality of the flesh,
bone and heart and eye.

Most never leave their mother.

Ovum Poem: Girl Meets Boy

She likes them young, energetic
not too intelligent –
born yesterday, in fact.

She enjoys the big
jostle, all that anonymous hedonistic head-
banging, but she won't take more than one
at a time, first come
first served, if she likes the thrust
of his argument.

He thinks it's just sex he's in for,
wags into one of many vulvas,
where he's sucked in, lies
a baby,
a crescent moon
in her breast,
infantile amphibious skin,
a sleeping salamander
drugged, devoured.

Once she's got what she wanted,
she can let herself go.
No more of that Evening In Paris shit,
whoring around in those short skirts, high heels,
sitting on the settee,
waiting for them to come.
Now she can get big, fat, globular,
dispense with men:

> "Bleed off ya bugger!
> Die you little whip-tailed beasties.
> Nobody's gonna fuck with me no more."

Chastity

Every look from her mother
is a nail into green wood,
clothes stapled to sapling limbs
keeping civilization upon her.

She combs leaves from her hair,
floats like Ophelia
the deadly nightshade of waterlilies,
ears under the river
face rimmed by water
eyes on the endless blue
night of eternity,
the tendons of her wrists slit.

She drifts with the silt,
rain damaged soil,
hair spreading in oil slick and rainbow
passing willow branches,
the stench of trains
ankles of muledeer
sound of car engines, jets.

She cannot grasp at men
or herself,
the folds in water.
She cannot grasp
the cavity
she is told is her centre,
the cavity
that must never be filled.

Five Women

Me and
five women with
five first babies
in a dining room
at a dinner with
pasta, bread, wine,
avocado salad,
bodies new and gushing
beside bodies drooping
soft alien motherness,
and the poop stories,
fart stories, how to
milk the legs of a child,
force the gas out, stories
of breast pumps,
talk of the high butterfat
of human milk, how it
separates in the glass bottles,
reminding them of the
churning of butter, of fetish,
of the new commercial nature,
market value of ova,
and the bringing forth of
ice cream from their own bodies,
never imagining they would ever
be thinking of such things.

And me, of course childless
and silent, my own
stories from the group home job –
Glen drops his pants to take a
crap in the park –
adult diapers, thrown dishes,
human scratches gone septic,
the bathing of long limbs,
the washing of hands:
not always ten fingers,
not always ten toes.

On the Rag

No squatting in a dark rush hut for her.
Cleopatra took over the Mediterranean world
in a fit of pre-menstrual syndrome
mowing down every Caesar in front of her,
blasting them with a hot sear of words
from a cannon disguised as a Persian carpet.

She wanted a man especially when she was on the rag,
switched to Mark Anthony, those army men
used to seeing blood on their swords.

Wait For It

I look at my watch and
wait for the gunshots,
the graveyard shift news,
lines scratched on my calendar
from Tuesday to Tuesday;
seven shootings this week
and more lives that are warheads.

Never with Kotex or tampon on hand,
under the car seat, in the purse,
I am a minor domestic disaster:
staining sheets, bicycle seat, skirt and slip
whenever God skewers me in the groin and
screams "Where is my woman?"

This burst of blood is not quite as shocking
as slick plastique explosives,
clear slice of knives,
intricacy of needle, kick,
the smooth impatient tongue of bullet,
but I make red.

Even post-war handbooks
told us to duck for the thousand
megatons expected someday, that
women
and men
should always be ready
to bleed.

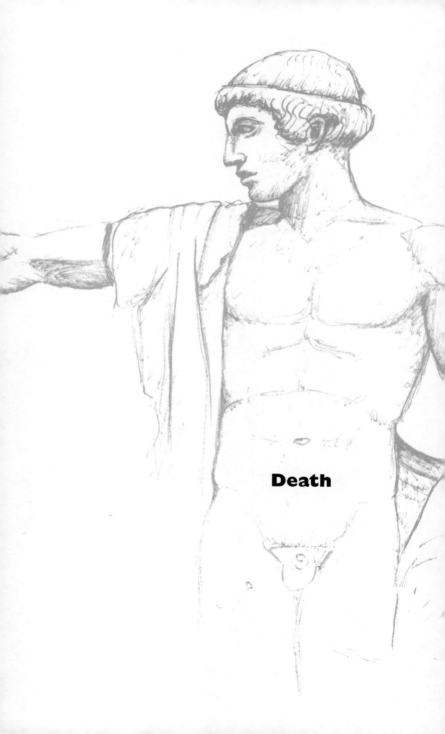

Death

Dragon Fly

Amelia Earhart, the heart
of an insect, humming
its silk and wood carapace,
shooting chrome through
holes shining in the air.

Days of sunlight punching her
face, light scatters the
sea, light in her teeth,
under her nails,
her tongue,
gulping it,
holding fire in her lungs,
hydrogen prominences
beat within her blood –
no shade between
woman and sun.

She must remind
herself to eat
food, drink water.
She is a body, has
weight, has forgotten
her feet,
curses the vortice of
sleep as un-
necessary and dangerous.

Turbulent, she
begins to bleed early
above the horse latitudes.
When she rises,
struggles with breeches,
cotton, glutted flow,
uterine tissue,
the wind tumbles
her hand from the throttle,
another dragon-
fly pouring its
life in the sky.

Old Woman With Wings

My Cossack Baba
flies over the prairie
on rainbow golden
wings of gothic angels,
searching the alleys,
dragging back cardboard
boxes of baby clothes,
bits of cars,
broken chairs,
to force on her grandchildren,
more to feed a vacuum of
Slavic hunger,
memories of serfdom,
the hold of a ship
walnut-shelling it
over the spastic waves,
reeking of whiskey and vomit.

Canada is a belly of bounty she
can't conform to, pushing bargain-
basement chocolate into my hands: white,
desiccating beneath the wrapper,
dumping Glad bags of smashed
radios in my car, refusal
impossible in my language,
so foreign to her.

She can't believe her luck
even before Chernobyl. Here,
nothing but grass between
two rivers and stars,
acres of dew and insects,
the sky a suspension
of funnels and vortices,
cyclones and dust devils,
slipping over gravel roads and stubble,
the invisible swirling of air
behind her wings.

She sees herself in bridal gown –
arranged marriage at the age of fifteen –
and aging into her ninth decade,
lace veil a streaming comet,
lands of drought showing
her skin in fissures and gullies,
the earth too dry to breathe water,
the mirror of her flight
long ago in the sea.

The Railroad in the 1950s

If only you would go mad, mother,
and be done with it. No more of these
diabolically plotted dinner parties,
the three square meals a day,
the shopping trips with gloves and
purse held in the crook of your arm,
church and parent-teacher meetings,
rows of cramped spinach,
brown butcher-wrapped meats in the freezer
labelled hysterically with a black wax pencil,
everything double, triple, quadruple bagged.
No more smiling or agreeing, hiding the bottle
or the weeping, the bad side effects,
the speeding, speeding always
on the rails

so I will never know you
just walking
in feet
bare, and your own.

Those rails, that lipstick, that smile, that house beautiful.
If you die
or get soul-stoned and suicide yourself
through a window into the Snake River Canyon
the train is still
going in the right direction,
good for another ten thousand miles.

Elegy for Maria

You may have only hours –
huddle of bones beneath granny squares,
nursing home blankets,
fog of cataracts,
fifty pounds of flesh lost to anorexia,
the righteous wasting of the old.

I read you stories until my eyes bleed,
your own words of you and
a house pinning the prairie,
a saline lake, crystal
shores of salt red and white
clouds of geese on the water,
the time the boat floated
away with baby Emma
in waves of rushes.

The two of you hitched
across the Depression,
slept in ditches, God's love
and safety, and a summer
picking cherries
from the top of a ladder –

a seemingly endless feast
of days
of red sweetness, the flesh
of life ecstatic
even so virginal as you remain.

Here, then, is your last meal,
aspiring writer:
three hours of narrative
bliss before death.

When

When she

the double-barrelled glans
of the shotgun in her mouth
her husband just striding
in from the field
the soup over-
boiling the stove, the baby
screaming high-chair stranded
in the plane-crash din
of the six-o'clock news

There in

the black-tilled garden of early spring
nothing growing yet
and the red-winged birds
about to shatter themselves
from the trees

St. Helen

In a triplet of maiden aunts
you snowbirded your way to Arizona,
went to church, ate at the smorgs,
waited tables (our Lady of Charity),
wandered the sunset desert in canvas sneakers
picking stones, filling bottles of sand,
bringing rock candy and mini-bibles
to adoring nephews and nieces
who wanted to be missionaries for your sake.

I saw you wasting on a foam pad
after your sisters brought you home
in the air ambulance, thin blue
veins flowing with murderous cells.

My memory of you is spectral, white-sheeted,
you ghost of my youngest Halloween,
creeping up my father's path
to push chocolate and oranges
into my frightened loving hands.

Women Keep Death

Peaceful in a meadow
of hospital linen and Russian print
flowers, pink and black, and black.
She lies in her own absence, in my presence.

Mother folds Grandma's hands, smoothes
sheets, soft woven crop of flax, cotton,
another woman keeping death
while our husbands lean dumb against the wall.

Mother combs the grey field
of her forehead, empty of self,
stone placed, grass grown,
hand over face,
lash of eye pricking her palm,
the weeds and nettles of loss,
as my mother closes her mother's eyes.

Skate

The boy who did it
was strange in the head
went on my bus
disappeared when I was eight.
Back then
you were lucky if you
found used skates that fit
your child-feet for a season.

My friends asked me
how I could do that,
swing to the Beatles
When I'm Sixty-Four,
slide, slice ice,
silver blade sharpened to the bone.

No one else would do
spins in the fourth-hand
skates of a murdered girl,
picked from the blade pile
in the hardware basement,
name gashed on the inside
leather – red jiffy marker –
head smashed by a shovel,
body in a ditch.

I did the waltz jump,
my first full revolution
cherry flip,
Laura's red name
searing my ankles.

The Humours Deranged

1.

I don't necessarily wear
my swastika every day,
carry my spear or blow-pipe,
but I always dress appropriately.
People don't always know who I am.

Sometimes, when the hostess
is exquisite in satin, and the mushroom
canapés are of a particular quality
I, in fact, unzip,
dangle my penis
into the martini,
suck it,
jam the olive up my anus.

The after-dinner speech
comes quite naturally. I
slide my tongue along
the dog ripples of my soft palate
down the wet bone of inner tooth,
pull back, slide
again, again,
further through the purse of my lips,
until semen spits
little jags and moans between my teeth.

I rest, urinate into the dessert dish, shake
my lips of the last droplet.

There is never applause.
My audience never applauds.

2.

Every month I take it
upon myself
to bleed
from my breasts.
Multinationals sell
two sanitary napkins,
not one,
and congratulate me.

Every three hours
I place my
baby on the tile
of a shopping mall,
gather my skirts,
squat and let the child suck
milk from my vulva
before I fling it
against the wall.
Before the police
siren their way
through the crowd.

3.

There are times, though, when I am
pale from vomiting blood, my
feces hard with abundant iron
corpuscles.

Bile creeps through
my arteries, clogged
with chewed meat
of indeterminate species.
Little bones catch in the bends
of my veins, capillaries –
splinter cuts
beneath my skin
swelling with yellow acid.

I can't staunch the flow within me,
every cell a shimmering agony.
I can't stop my ears from the grind
of knuckle and cartilage deep
where they say my heart has forgotten.

Maiming off my own fingers, ears,
will not suffice
to stop the pain.
Bullets in my brain,
blighted ether in my lungs,
my eyes blinded with embered sticks,
giving only my own
body to be burned
in annihilation of being

will not suffice,

but there are billions of others.

Where You Are Taking Me

Where are you taking me?

You drive your father's car.
You're forty-two
and I'm twenty-four,
only a twist of your age.
The radio turns itself on
and you hit the dash with your fist;
you stop the music with a violence.

So the other drivers are bastards, are they?

Well, maybe they are.

I look out at the bundled mountain biker
who passes us in the traffic,
tearing away at the whiteness
of the snow.

I wish I were as cold.

The frost and the tears
freeze his eyelashes together

and I envy him this also.

Running

A swallow kamikazes into the glass
and I find him dead in the window box
among the pinks –
astonishing to grow pure colour,
oranges, peaches, fuschias.

We build holes in the pavement
for trees to grow through,
lights to wink at flying men
from the top of office towers
so 747s don't shatter the flakes
of silica that keep the wind
from our accountants.

We walk into doors and walls,
are broken by the impact of cars,
semi-trailer trucks, meteors
of space junk, electrons
fired from screens glowing
the color of aluminum.
We pour cement where
olives and columbine could grow.

And yet we know its unholiness –
the untouchable concrete.
I will not walk it with bare supplicant feet,
but armour myself with
technological incantations
of rubber, plastic,
pods of air and oil,
protecting even the lowest
parts of my body
from what I have done.

Breasts and Carcinogens

1.

In a crumpled magazine
waiting for my cancer test
I see another squatting Venus
in the British Museum:
marble eye without a pupil, a
Greek maiden
preparing herself for a
cold Victorian bath.

Sixteen hours a day
a corset cramps her belly,
atrophies back and stomach,
ensures her death in childbirth.

The solid leg
articulate feet,
the grace of her breast
peeping, an eye
from under folded arms.

2.

The shape of nipples through my sweater.

My breast is the face beneath
the dance of the seven veils

confined for the muslim safety of
men, confined with the

Bermuda Triangle
medusic snake hair between my thighs.

Even though men have their own nipples.

It's a scientific fact
they could lactate with practice,
squeeze out white nourishment
for their children.

3.

I don't do this trick often
except in hospital rooms
when the white gowns look
too angelic:

undo clasp through shirt,
snake hand up arm,
pull strap down around hand,
flip the spandex
out the other sleeve.

I release flesh within
clothes, shape shift.
What does their precise form matter
varied with pads, underwire,
cross my heart?

Why do I strap these glands down?
A mere fashion of topiary,
clipped shrubs,
rounded, pointed in the sixties,
madonnaesque,
confinement
maddening the cells.

4.

A knot of hopelessness
above my heart.

When my friend found
the lump, two o'clock
in my left breast,
we looked naked at each other.
So much airless space
between us.

The intern inserts
his long needle
sucks up some fluid,
comes back smiling.
Fibril adenoma.
Benign.

But keep watching for signs of change.

Prairie Woman

1.

I once existed and looked like this
among sleigh tracks
and children
angel-falling in the snow.

Here is my husband,
his winter-beaten face,
the hands he wore in the summer.

His eyes are transparent.
I see the horizon through them:
ice-blue, floury with snow.

In the spring
the snow will mingle
with the earth
and he will love me.

2.

Help me here, my daughter.
Roll up my sleeves,
tie the apron,
leaven the earth
with oats.
Hide straw in it
and sand
a new leaf
and a damsel fly.

Then I awake at the window
and the sun pierces me.

She was my girl who died
beneath the willows,
stormed sightless
in the cold.
We kept her under the snow
until spring

yet I see her flying
her spirit white in the poplars
like a blown sheet.

Are you sleep-waiting little one?
I am baking fresh.
In a slow season
you will have bread of the earth.

Fear of Life Taken

My father pushed
a knife into earth
he thought he owned,
pulled out a garden
ringed with poppies,
white hens flocking
to my arms,
the wind in the grass in my hair.

My seven sisters
dressed in the same pattern
of child
and womanhood
and sky
and church
Gideon's trumpets
and shepherd's crooks
in a land without lambs
and fewer buffalo
and those darker
people by the river.

I grew peonies
baked cakes
shucked corn.
My husband shot deer
helped make my babies
filled coffee cans with arrowheads
after he walked behind the plow,
lay in his coffin so obediently
at the funeral when his hands
had never been so cold.

He bequeathed me to the world, to
hospitals and age and sickness,
the joints of thought loose,
body falling
to the mercy of a defibrillator,
greased electric paddles
slapping my heart alive.

I thought it was the Cree
come to get me at last, fulfill
the wild west – fear
the price of empty acres –
chasing me from my life,
the stolen land, my heart
beating beneath
sheets so white.

Leaving the Land / Memory

She wades in the wheat, thinking
if the sun bursts with pain
in the field

> it will rain flax
> clothe the angels in linen
> and the utterness of life.
> The dog leaps from the hay to his hand.

This was the place he most wanted to be
when he lived, and he's still
here in her mourning.

> The waltz of her man, seeding.
> She is his wife in his arms
> and will remember this day

but she can't dance
with a dead man.

> It is his hand in the wind
> picket fencing
> along the white bones
> of birch,

lightning to crack
the sky's blue porcelain.

De Medici

1.

Fog eats the hills.
Catherine, anorexic daughter
of rag-trade merchants,
takes a cab from Florence to
the Ile de France,
stands contrapposto
at the lip of a wine bar
to meet princes.

She winds her legs with Vaseline and cling-wrap
when she models for the agencies, the runway,
takes up cigarettes, absinthe,
a French waiter with Moorish eyes, stubble,
an aspiring painter.

They are Kouros and Kore.

"How men will love
the turning away of your neck," he says.
"There were days when men could not bear
the eyes of women upon them
even in death."

2.

He paints her naked,
tells her to avert her eyes
from his mind, to look instead
at the ochre stain on his smock
above the groin, spin
back to the Renaissance
when every cock
was the worm of death,
bloating her with humanity
and plagues.

"Downcast your eyes.
It's not your lips that smile,
not your eyes, but your skin.
Snake your neck back.
Your arms are wings.
Let them open your breast
and air and eyes will fly around you
forever.
Feel the lust of a thousand
unborn men flutter upon your breast.

"You see what the painting will say?
I don't want you.
I want you.
Here is the thread
to take me with."

He paints her naked
with names:
rose madder, maddened rose,

raw sienna, burnt sienna,
lamp black, viridian,
raw umber, green earth,
and she is addicted,
bound by her image.

At the first exhibition
she becomes a present in oils,
her own dowry, wrapped for
the Dauphin (who was
always pulling the strings).

3.

It's not as if marriage took a lot out of her.

She meets Watteau, aging
into the Enlightenment.
He wants her to gain a little weight,
practice the dimpled
pink-bummed fling
into the ruffles of a rhododendron.

She becomes known as
the patron with the silk arse
and the silver purse.
There is a sculptor
she fascinates herself with
who forms the dead
into tombstones,
rips the tendons from corpses
to see where they go,
keeps pale hands
under his bed.

He observes how the outer
feminine genitalia
resemble the human ear.

He could speak of things
he'd like to do to her body
but they would deafen her.

4.

She dies at eighty-five.
The Dauphin lays her effigy in the Louvre
on a lascivious bed of marble.
Here, she offers herself
finally for total consumption,
naked to seduce the dead, the statues,
men who have a taste for thin girls,
old girls with corded necks,
straining to look away from
the decay that strips bodies of sex, of
the delicacy of breast and testicle.

There she is among the Fragonards, the
Cabanels. Forced to keep the same
bad company as she did in life. At least
she didn't heat the sheets of the Spaniard.
Picasso was a bastard, but no one can
tell a woman that, unless she also
dresses her hands with graphite,
has her own bones and brushes,
turns her body to charcoal and
scrapes herself along a white plaster wall.

5.

Was this the long vacation of
life? she thinks,
her history of art?
Now, back to business.
The states of death and pre-conception
make little difference.
An infinite number of people
do not exist at the Louvre
and this is one of them.

Sure, she had some good times, too,
which might not be so clear,
gazing on her stone portrait of decomposition,
the object men have made her,
still life with words:
exhaustion

death

I don't want you

I want you

Naked Men

Nude Model

He takes too long
to put on his robe.

A beard clothes his face
feet ground with chalk
the dust of burned wood.
He wanders as they finish
iris, belly, pectorals,
inkwash the background
smudge black.

There are many versions of him. He
leans over shoulders, looks
for their eyes, speaks, but

the young women who have
drawn his testicles with charcoal
are too intimate with his body
to speak to him.

Freud as Adam

Whiplash from a branch
of the tree of life
breaks his spectacles
as he follows Eve
too closely
through the garden.

She slaps him when he calls her Mama.

He names the snake a symbol
and is bitten
on his ring finger

then comforts himself on a couch of grass
getting oedipal with Mother Earth
thinking of Viennese coffee
envying his descendants
their possibilities for patricide.

He doesn't know all women will
think he's an asshole.

He wouldn't give a fuck.

That Angel Michael Buonarroti With His Red Lamborghini

1.

He was wise to be born
Italian, if only for the leather.
They don't tell the fifteen year olds
he liked the blue feather boas,
the orange four-inch
platform shoes in the naughty
boutiques, didn't really hate
Leonardo, but invited him
for gelato in the piazza
of Santa Maria Novella,
their rivalry nothing
but thwarted lovers quarrels.

What else could he have thought of,
lying on his back for two
years, arm's length
from the Chapel ceiling,
caressing paint
into heroic muscle?

2.

A man in the London underground
with classical nose and thick brow,
red ram's-wool hair warming
half his length of vertebrae,
a body Mick would love
to sculpt, touching the ice of
marble if he couldn't
have the freckled flesh.

A train hurls past and the man throws
his hair into the path of running
commuters as he grinds
the corduroy body of his lover
against a wall,
a Plexiglas advertisement for panty-
hose.

3.

Mick saw the Jesus flow of Albrecht
Dürer's hair: ringletted cascade, mahogany,
only a print, a sheet of electrons,
Albrecht advertising his
body on the net,
supermodel of the Renaissance.

Mick almost picks up the phone, sends an e-mail.
A long distance liaison would be better
than this rivalry, vicarious for
burning, for a man who doesn't even
know his own hand
on the closet door.

See the castratti? Mick says to Leo
as they take a turn about the church,
arm in arm, as the fashion would have it.
Listen to them sing. They have lost nothing.

Leonardo licks his cone, has his doubts.
Vroom says the Lamborghini.
Mick leaves him doubting
in a spray of terra-cotta dust.

Italian widows, businessmen,
watch while kneeling,
black kerchiefs and rosaries,
blue ties, the London Times,
know how impossible it is
not to love a man,
condemn them anyway.

The False Dawn of Mechanics

Vulcan was an old coot
but he had the shoulders for it,
hammered out
all those Olympian horse shoes –
shod the sun horses of Apollo
(Go, man, go!)
see who gets to bed first,
and with Venus as his wife
there was no contest
until the day he thought
maybe it'll get harder
if I stick it in the fire.

Plato as Adam

Pornography warps a man's mind. On the street, he can't
help imagining them bent over chairs with stilettos until
his religious conversion as a computer graphics designer.

Women are only shadows of the ideal. In that pantyhose
commercial, he fed symbols through the keyboard and
stretched her legs by thirty percent, a seven-foot tall
freak who looked good only when she was lying down.

He knows it's all trivia. After all, what is pantyhose in
the great scheme of Things? We are more than eighty-
five percent water, then a thin mud of trace minerals.
We are animals.
We are atom child.
We are electricity.
Not to worry about angels and the smell of plums, the
thought of smile and moon and soil.
If it seems good, it is always better somewhere else.

He sends naked pictures of himself over the internet –

not to worry –

only vibrations in silica,
a shadow of the ideal,

some part of his body elongated...

The Tyger

1.

In the National Gallery of London
beneath Puvis de Chavannes'
The Beheading of John the Baptist
the man recited The Tyger.

Tyger, Tyger, burning bright
like the selfishness of that bitch
who left me to become famous in New York.

We used to walk the gallery here,
she with her sketchbook, like you,
drawing the men as if she'd created them,
princes, bastards, all condemned under her pen.

I put my book down, see
his nails, long and white, cutting
into the palm of his hand.

2.

He calls himself a black romantic poet,
tends bar in Hastings,
came here for the multitude
purposes of self pity.

He sits too close to me, an attempt
to belong to her again.
Do you think I'm drunk? he says,
gets up and leaves
(the last time I ever see him)
as I sketch dark Israeli hair
ancient robe and loincloth, the arm
straining, power slung.

The executioner has drawn back his sword.
John the Baptist waits in perpetuity
to be severed again and again
in the minds of the living.

The Popes as Adam

1.

They lock the apple in a golden reliquary
with the pubis of Saint Teresa of Avila,
savaged by the Holy Ghost
in the habit of her spirit.

They get off on a technicality,
not eating the apple, just
screwing it into a socket of earthly light.

2.

Little pink popes dancing in new dresses
with satin skull caps and ballet slippers
in the perpetual dew of Eden,

collecting artefacts.

Polaroids of breath whooping
from their mouths in squalls
of utopian mist,
a vial filled with the
blood of the circumcision of Christ.

On the shelf above the refrigerator
is the curled rind of God's foreskin
in a mayonnaise jar.

Love letters. Objects of passion.
The stub of a candle, the pen from a
hotel room, a ring. Cherished,
most likely to be burned in
times of awakening and illusion.

3.

Innocent and Pius were good little boys
for Our Father Who Art In Heaven.
Burn those Albigensians, Anabaptists,
idols and witches and heretics.
Burn that firewood beneath my concubine.
Lock Galileo in his observatory;
there are penalties for accuracy.

Tend my garden said the Lord,
but the popes were never much
into bending and sweating,
never learned to eat their vegetables,
preferred chicken,
preferred soft trussed
Italian mistresses to Eve,
who was only naked,
had not the mystery of lingerie
and plucked foreheads,
oyster tongued
women to slide down their throats.

This, they thought, must be paradise.

Atlas Held Aloft in the Heavens by a Green Orange
(A Modern Fairy Tale)

I am the man with no neck.

I am the man who lifts the weights
with no neck.

I am the man who builds my pecs
who lifts the weights
with no neck.

I am the man who flashes my butt
who builds my pecs
who lifts the weights
with no neck.

I am the man who wiggles my cock
who flashes my butt
who builds my pecs
who lifts the weights
with no neck.

I am the man who slithers with oil
who wiggles my cock
who flashes my butt
who builds my pecs
who lifts the weights
with no neck.

You are the women.

Rutting Season at the Café

On Sundays, the cooks go into
rutting season. The hair on their chests
curls glossy, drops into
bacon and eggs.

They stomp around,
fight with the Canadian girls
they hired to serve
who won't sleep with them
because their brains have accents,

eyes greasing over short skirts,
black pantyhose, thick grabbing
hands scarred with the melting
metal pans of lasagna, deep frying fat,
teeth wet with insistence.

"Tired? Too much taka taka last night?"
they demand, a violent hope, as

the women butter toast,
take searing plates of eggs
naked-handed to the church
people at the tables,
having discovered a kitchen
in which women don't belong.

Adam, You Little Devil

He would have had a Hell of a job
getting Eve to go first.
Bite that Apple.
Or was it an apricot?

The fang of his anger came when he knew
he couldn't just infiltrate and slither away.
He had to walk around in this naked disguise;
there's nothing worse than a devil with goose bumps,
a chill, the flu.
He should have slipped into the snake.
Not this.
Not perfect human form.
Not gardening,
for Christ's sake.

"After you, my darling," he winds up wheedling,
teeth green because vegetables don't agree with him.
Neither do breadfruit, pomegranates,
mandarins, pecans.
He wants devil's food.
Hot wings.
Bats.

When he finally gets down to it,
the Temptation In The Garden,
Eve would rather have sex than pears,
but all he can do is sneeze, search
for the baser elements, for
cayenne in the harvest,
go careering up the local volcano
to fling himself in.

He was a virgin, you know.

Waitress Honesty

Today's specials are chicken Kiev and pepper steak. The soup,
we call cream of fucking mushroom, and it's good today
because it's winter and the cooks aren't shedding chest hair.

You have a choice of potato, baked, mashed, fries, spaghetti
or rice, and then there's the dressing – if you'd seen several
gallons of Thousand Island in a vat, a thick soup the
colour of skin, you'd pass by, believe me.

If you order toast, chances are we'll drop it on the floor,
butter it and bring it out anyway, and they use some
chemical to keep the ancient salad from turning brown. I
don't recommend the salad.

I see you laughing. You think it's funny. If you slap your
child one more time I'll call the police, even if it gets me
fired. I'll pour a long thin barb of coffee into your lap, break
your back over the edge of the booth if your hand meets his
small face again, if it amuses you to see him cry.

Will there be anything else?

Bathing N

You don't have to dream of geishas,
of being waited upon hand and foot
tooth and nail
by servants,
women who'll do just about anything.

I've clipped your toenails
cut your hair
brushed your teeth
wiped your bum
worked suntan lotion
into the lotus folds of your ear
aimed your penis into the toilet.
You have bitten me on a whim
and I have mingled the wound
with blood and peroxide and
lifted you up again.

At thirty, your skin is almost new:
feet don't walk
forehead doesn't worry
hands don't work
mouth has no words
but moans
squinting sunsmiles
screams without understanding
of toothache, migraine.

The public health nurse lectures me
and the other young women.
Pull back the foreskin.
Clean around the glans.
Don't be too shy to dry it well.
Wear rubber gloves.

Erections make a tent in your pajamas.
I bundle your pee-sodden bedclothes to the laundry
put my hands under your arms
move you to your chair
then the toilet, where
somehow you squeeze out the semen
lacking the use of hands:
a virgin birth.

You like the bath
slap your palm on the water
flap wet fingers
laugh at the dollop of
suds I put on your nose.

Lying on your back
limbs curled in the air
there is no shame of your body,
of what it does
and does not do.
The vortice of your flesh,
your completeness, even
your happiness terrifies me.
How can I allow for
my own discontent?

We sit later.
I stir your consciousness
into the bowl of your hand
with the chafe of my nails.
It is the only sensuality
you will get from another
And I am paid well for it.

Darwin as Adam

You want me to be who?
To go *where?*
Why not Atlantis instead?
Or if I must be mythological
let me appear in the heavens
as a goldfinch by the constellation Cygnus.

Or maybe I'll be that Saint – let me
preach – no – sing to my finches:

> I am St. Frances
> poor boy of Assisi.
> Give me the stigmata
> of the Holy Spirit.

> Fill your seed beaks with flesh
> bore holes in my palms
> the tendoned arches of my feet.
> Fly through my orifices
> my ears, my eyes, my mouth
> you shafts of enlightenment.

How was that?
Religious enough for you?

Fine.

Don't you offer me some tart in the shrubbery.
I am British.

The Son Forsaken in The Garden

Thought he was Peter Pan
like any kid named Jesus.
Climbed the trees with arms
to lie in, the cedars of Lebanon,
but he'd even hug a pine,
ladder his way through the spiral branches
needles like thorns, scraping the
bark against his warm black-skinned cheek.

He taunted his father from the orchard.
"I'm never coming down!
I will live off peaches and pears
and rose petals, any cluster
of grapes that vine their way toward me.

I will keep your watch
wing my eyes over the horizon
to story you with thunder and lightning
stampedes of impala and wildebeest."

So Jesus hung there among the apples
ripening into his thirties
until that first strange woman gazed up
slid a warm hand around his genitals.

the begatitudes

it is written

adam begat seth
seth begat enos begat cainan
begat and so on
isaac begat jacob
begat obed begat jesse
the first six or more
scenes of our little
blue movie (dolly in
dolly out dolly in dolly out)
the multigenerational
orgies of the testaments
endless family tree
of dicks and haunches
and fuckings
men grunting on sand
striped with sun and
bedouin lucence

and somewhere in the dark
somewhere
the dark-skinned pierce-nosed
women travailing
with the blood
and joy of newborn
behind the purdah of words

Him in the Sky

My eyes hovered on horses,
wheat grass flying
under the wheels of the school bus,
hot finger drawings and our breaths
opening on frosted windows.

At school we were unsaddled,
galloping through recess and canyon,
I, Black Beauty, you, the White Stallion
bursting through the lilacs and soccer
games, barrel-racing the maples.

You wanted to lead me along
for the ride, were certain we'd be
raptured to heaven
before blood and boys,
Jesus telling you it would be
better than all this to die.

You were a girl of the advent,
a child before puberty, and with God –
Him there in the sky
with the four horsemen –
drunken flying striking
match after match,
igniting the ripe fields
of rye and salvation.

My Sister, My Spouse

You are allowed to read the Song of Solomon
allowed to interpret it
as the love of Christ for His Church:

> I am the rose of Sharon
> the lily of the valley
> your dove
> your undefiled one.

> How fair is thy love
> my sister, my spouse.

You would not tell me what whore meant
when you were a boy and I was a girl
and there were no other children
for miles, for years.
I watched you pee in the grass.
You told me babies come from urine
and I believed you,
my sandbox parent
snowball parent
spikenard and saffron
calamus and cinnamon
crabapple and chokecherry.

Just try to be in the same room
with me then, with our parents.
I won't say
a thing.
Not even hello.
I won't mention again
that passage in the Pentateuch where
women are commanded to marry

their rapists. I won't
demonstrate the happiness
you think is so blasphemous
without Jesus.
I won't ask
for apology
or explanation
for these five brotherless years.

Remember who loved you?

But you defeat me.
I can't even speak of you,
can hardly write this.
If you had whispered
"my sister, my spouse,"
it might explain such abandonment
even as it sickened us both,
if you had admitted you were too close
for your faith
to bear the movement
of my mind.

Remember when you said
you would have put yourself away
with bullet or pill
if Christ hadn't re-born you?

I remember.

Don't be afraid
precious life.

I won't call you.

My Father As Adam / Ancestral Memories of The Garden

He would ask God about grafting,
name the bark, sap layer, pith,
ask for a penknife.

                Swallows breathe with their wings.

He cleaves branches like hooves,
surgeons one amputated apple twig
to the stump of another.

                Roses grow up through the lilacs,
                bend fireworking blossoms
                in rising heat, day.

Norland, crab, Sunnybrook, then
apricot, nectarine, profusions of limbs
that grow together, miraculous.

                The pine keeps a heart of grackles.

I am Eve running barefoot
to get twine from his workshop
in all days of innocence.

                Wind blows. The tree of
                life is a thousand wings
                without the mind for flight.

Acknowledgements

I gratefully acknowledge the following publications which first printed versions of the poems specified below:

The Antigonish Review, "The Tyger," Autumn, 1996.

Canadian Literature, "De Medici," Winter, 1997.

The Capilano Review, "Mae West Does Eve" ("Eve"), "Freud as Adam," "Adam, You Little Devil," "The Popes as Adam," "My Father as Adam / Ancestral Memories of the Garden," Fall, 1996.

CV2, "Where You Are Taking Me," Winter, 1994, "Bathing N," and "Waitress Honesty," Spring 1997.

Envoi (Stoke-on-Trent, England), "Olympia," October, 1997.

Event, "Darwin as Adam," ("Darwin in the Heavens") Winter, 1997.

The Fiddlehead, "Skate," Winter, 1997.

Global Tapestry Journal (Lancs., England), "Mae West Does Eve" ("Eve").

Grain, "Prairie Woman," and "First Apple," Winter, 1991.

The Malahat Review, "Leaving the Land / Memory," Fall, 1997.

The New Quarterly, "The False Dawn of Mechanics," Fall, 1997.

NeWest Review, "Running," December 1997/January 1998.

Prairie Fire, "Old Woman With Wings," Spring, 1997.

Vintage 97, Anthology of The League of Canadian Poets contest, "Red Neck Love."

Thanks to Geoffrey Ursell, Barbara Sapergia, Elizabeth Philips and Duncan Campbell for support in both literary and visual fun. Thanks also to the poets of the Saskatchewan Writers Guild for keeping the old brain cells zapping, and forever thanks to Colin.

about the author

Bernice Friesen is a writer and visual artist who was born in Rosthern, Saskatchewan, and now divides her time between Saskatoon and Hornby Island in British Columbia.

Her fiction, poetry and juvenile fiction have been published in numerous periodicals, such as *Grain, CV2, Prairie Fire* and *The Capilano Review,* and anthologies such as *eye wuz here, The Landmarks,* and *Vintage '97.* Her juvenile novel, *The Seasons are Horses,* was a finalist for two Saskatchewan Book Awards.

Her visual art, in addition to being featured on the covers of Coteau's *Open-Eye* poetry series this year, has been cover and interior art for several other books and periodicals.

Bernice has degrees in both Education and Printmaking from the University of Saskatchewan.

THE OPEN EYE POETRY SERIES:

Poetry that knows where you live!

Check out the rest of the titles in the 1998 Open Eye series:

My Flesh the Sound of Rain
Heather MacLeod

A masterpiece of native and white myth and icon – an Indian shaman shares attention with the Christian Virgin and the pagan holy days Beltain and Samhain.

Second Skin
Jeanne Marie de Moissac

Poetry born of an attachment to earth's abundance – children, animals both domestic and wild, plants and stones of the rural landscape.

A slow dance in the flames
Lynda Monahan

Deeply in love with language – celebrates the perfection of nature as well as the imperfect, painful, but often alluring state of being human.

COTEAU BOOKS